The Balloon Adventure

Written by Mary-Anne Creasy

Illustrated by Chantal Stewart

Flying Start
to Literacy®

Contents

Chapter 1
Big news on the farm

None of the animals at the farm liked Flash the racehorse. He was always boasting about how famous he was and how many races he had won.

"Look at all my ribbons," said Flash, as he pranced around the farm.

The other farm animals tried to ignore Flash, but they were annoyed by his boasting.

One morning the rooster was
very excited.

"The King and Queen are coming
today!" he crowed.

"They must be coming to see me,"
said Flash proudly.

"No, they are coming to see a huge balloon fly in the sky for the first time ever," said the sheep. "I heard the farmer telling his wife."

Soon the animals saw the King and Queen and a huge crowd of people arriving at the farm.

The animals watched as a large, flat balloon was dragged into the field. It was made from pieces of cloth that were held together with nearly two thousand buttons.

Two men began to build a fire. They held the opening of the balloon over the fire. The balloon began to puff up.

It got bigger and bigger until the
huge balloon was filled with
hot air.   Then it started to float.

Chapter 2

All aboard

"And now, we need some people to ride in our balloon," said one of the men. "They will be the very first people to fly."

The King suddenly shouted out, "No! People are not allowed to fly in that balloon until we know it is safe. We will use animals."

All the farm animals except for
Flash listened in shock.

"I am sure they will ask me to fly
in the balloon," said Flash to the
other animals.

Flash saw his chance. He tried to jump into the basket under the balloon. But the farmer quickly grabbed him and pulled him away.

"What are you doing, you stupid horse?" said the farmer. "You can't go up in a balloon. You might be killed, and you make me a lot of money. I will put in some worthless animals."

The farmer pointed to the sheep,
the duck and the rooster who
were standing nearby.

But the sheep, the duck and the rooster
did not want to go in the balloon.

"Help! Help!" said the sheep, as she
tried to run away.

"Let me go!" quacked the duck,
as he flapped his wings.

"No, no, no!" crowed the rooster
as loudly as he could.

But it was no use. The farmer grabbed the animals and tossed them into the balloon.

Before the frightened animals could jump out, the ropes tying the balloon to the ground were cut. The balloon slowly floated high into the air.

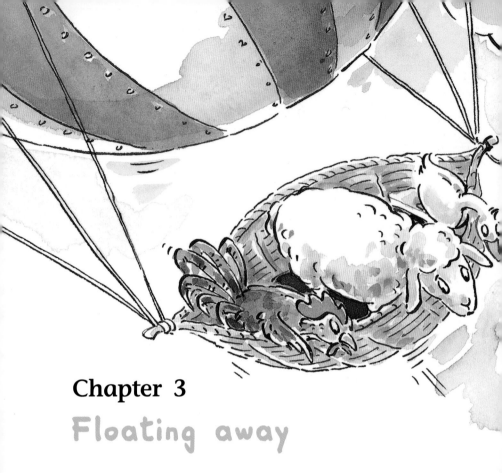

Chapter 3

Floating away

As the animals floated higher, they became more and more frightened. The sheep, the duck and the rooster looked over the side of the basket and watched as their farm got smaller and smaller.

But even as they drifted away they could still see Flash's face. He looked very cross as he watched them and he stamped his hoofs on the ground.

"We must get down," said the sheep.

"But how?" asked the duck.

The sheep looked around the basket.
Then she looked up into the balloon.

"Look," she said. "This balloon is held together with lots of buttons. If we could get some of those buttons off, it would make a hole and let some of the hot air out."

"Good idea," said the rooster.

Chapter 4

Down to earth

The duck and the rooster
flew up and pecked off some
of the buttons. This made a small
hole in the balloon. Hot air began
to leak out of the hole and the
balloon began to sink.

Down, down, down it floated, right down to the ground where it landed with a bump.

The animals tumbled out onto the grass where they lay gasping and shaking.

Then they heard cheering and shouting.
A crowd ran to the animals. The people
cheered the animals as they carried
them high in the air.

When the King and Queen arrived, they insisted on the animals riding in their coach. They took them back to the palace for a huge celebration.

And that is how the sheep, the duck and the rooster became famous all around the world. They were the first living things to fly in a hot-air balloon.

After that, Flash never said another word about being the most famous animal on the farm.